Beloved Stranger

Reflections on Mental Illness

by

Mary Brust Heaney

Proctor Publications, L.L.C. • Ann Arbor, Michigan • USA

Library of Congress Catalog Card Number: 95-72875

ISBN: 1-882792-19-X

Printed in the United States of America

"Mental health problems do not affect three or four out of every five persons, but one out of one."
Dr. William Menninger

Dedicated to the families and friends of the mentally ill, who know the anguish and bewilderment of a loved one becoming a stranger to them. Daily they negotiate the perplexing maze of mental illness. Their stories are here. They are the living testimony that "Mental health problems do not affect 3 or 4 out of every 5 persons, but one out of one."

The stories contained herein are composites of typical true personal experiences with names and details changed to preserve anonymity.

ACKNOWLEDGMENTS

I want to thank my husband, Dr. Joseph A. Heaney, for sharing so generously with me his experience and expertise. To my children, Joseph III, Kathleen, Stephen, Clare, Michael, and Patrick, I say thanks for being a source of encouragement and inspiration.

Also, I am grateful to LaRae Giese Heaney for her assistance in proof reading and to my publisher, Hazel Proctor and her staff for their help and confidence throughout. Lastly, I deeply appreciate the artwork contributed by my daughter, Clare Heaney Thompson.

"HOPE IS THE THING WITH FEATHERS
THAT PERCHES IN THE SOUL
AND SINGS THE TUNE WITHOUT THE WORDS
AND NEVER STOPS – AT ALL –
AND SWEETEST IN THE GALE IS HEARD"

EMILY DICKINSON

INTRODUCTION

My contact with mental illness for twenty-five years has been not so much with mentally ill persons as with their families and caregivers. I have observed and listened, been impressed and been moved by their words and by their silences, in my psychiatrist-husband's waiting room, on the phone, in mental hospitals, and in the literature which graces our dining room table.

I have heard the wretched defensiveness of parents who feel accused of causing their child's illness. I have seen marriages falter under the stress of living with a mentally ill spouse or relative. I have glimpsed the debilitating shame, anguish and loneliness of young people with a mentally ill parent or sibling.

Over the years, books which educate, instruct, and address these issues have appeared. However, what strikes me as being crucial is the way we view our circumstances. The attitude we take towards the illness underlies and alters the assistance and information available to us. The bias of everyone's attitude helps or hinders, consoles or disheartens, invigorates or incapacitates. It colors our collective perception. I wrote this book to heighten awareness of the redemptive power in cultivating an attitude, above all, of hope.

I am neither a therapist nor an expert. And this book is not intended to teach or inform in any comprehensive way. The questions which haunted me through the years have always been, "Who nurtures the caregivers? Who encourages and appreciates them? Who comforts the beleaguered?" Thus, this book is an embrace, a handclasp, a salute to those families and caregivers who daily "weather the storm".

SECTIONS

 *HEARTACHE*

**"I'VE SEEN SO MANY CHANGEFUL YEARS,
ON EARTH I AM A STRANGER GROWN;
I WANDER IN THE WAYS OF MEN,
ALIKE UNKNOWING AND UNKNOWN."**

ROBERT BURNS
*Lament for James,
Earl of Glencairn*

> *"Which of us knows his brother? Who has looked*
> *at his father's heart? Which of us is not forever a*
> *stranger and alone....."*
>
>   **Thomas Wolf, <u>Look Homeward Angel</u>**

Only in bits and pieces and intermittent snatches of time do we know each other. There will be a sudden glint of comprehension when your eye catches mine, a laugh spontaneous and transparent that comes from deep within you. I catch a glimpse before you fade into the inscrutable mist of your private world. I am alone again and so are you. Like shooting stars these flashes of recognition link us, their light stored in memory. In the rare flicker of recognition, I know you are there under the mask of mental illness, and you know that I know. That makes all the difference.

Even though we may be strangers to one another much of the time, and know each other in only a haphazard and intermittent way, our aloneness is never complete; our mutual influence never lost.

> *"Everything that lives,*
> *Lives not alone, nor for itself."*
>
>   **William Blake**

"Your children are not your children, they are the
sons and daughters of life's longing for itself...And
though they are with you they belong not to you."
K. Gibran

My daughter is not my daughter. She lives in a world forever
closed to me, which I can never share, although I can get glimpses
of it now and then. As she sank into illness, I denied and chal-
lenged; tried to tug and shake her free, force her to be the person I
once thought I knew. It is not in my power. She has been given
to me for a time, but she is illusive as a moonbeam. Her thoughts
flutter and take flight like autumn leaves in a November wind.
She is part of a cosmic plan I cannot fathom. Who am I to
denounce it? I too am enmeshed in this mystery called life. If
even normal children "belong not to us" how much truer for
mentally ill children. How poignantly they live this truth.

"You may house their bodies but not their souls.
For their souls dwell in the house of tomorrow
where you cannot visit, not even in your dreams."
K. Gibran

*"Passing stranger, you do not know how longingly
I look upon you..."*
                                                    Walt Whitman

The most disconcerting thing about my husband's illness is that
he is normal and well functioning for long periods of time. Then
the atmosphere becomes ominous, like the oppressive green-black
sky that presages a tornado. A torrent of insults pours over the
dinner table. I experience a lightning jolt when the storm strikes.
But I have slowly learned to quickly distance myself before I start
feeling too badly, knowing it won't help at all to let this storm
buffet me. What is the sense of getting my feelings hurt, only to
have him feel guilty and bewildered after the episode subsides?
Now that he is on medication, the manic episodes are milder and
less frequent.

**The next best thing to being taken seriously is to NOT be taken
seriously! People with manic-depressive illness can enjoy long
bouts of normalcy during which they can function at a high level.
No mood can last forever, and time has a way of bringing about
change, so that inexorably another mood state will take over.
Remembrance of the recurring normal times can help us get
through the passing storms.**

"To everything there is a season
A time to weep and a time to
laugh..."
Ecclesiastes

Dear Diary, Mom's moods are unpredictable and extreme. To-
night she is having another big, really awful fight with Marie.
She is yelling because Marie did not do the dishes when she was
told. Marie screams, "I hate you, you horrible thing." It seems
like Mom's bad moods are getting worse. She can be perfectly
normal one week and we have fun together, and then she becomes
manipulative, paranoid and belligerent. That's what is confusing,
the on and off moods. She says we teenagers are driving her nuts
and we deliberately provoke her. I think Dad is scared of her.
Maybe we should move; Mom hates this neighborhood.

Eight years after I wrote this in my diary, Mom was diagnosed as
having manic depressive illness. She is on lithium and our lives
are so much less chaotic I can hardly believe it. We are beginning
to be able to separate the person from the behavior. We know she
has an illness. Her diagnosis is the best thing that's happened to
us. We don't keep searching for whatever in the environment
may have caused this latest outburst.

**Why does it take so long to find out what's wrong? The average
length of time manic-depressive illness goes undiagnosed or
misdiagnosed is eight years. With increasing knowledge we can
hope that this time line is shortened. Meanwhile, we learn to
relinquish the urge to fit life into neat schedules. We learn to
value the cycle of all events as they unfold, and appreciate that
there is a time for everything under the sun.**

"Can I see another's woe, and not be in sorrow, too? Can I see another's grief, and not seek kind relief?"

Wm. Blake

I cringe when Mom yells at Peggy. Mom thinks she is deliberately stubborn. Dad keeps harping on her school work and tries to get arithmetic into her head. His voice gets louder and louder and his face turns beet red. Why won't she learn? "Why doesn't she have friends, Jane, like you?" they say to me. I feel sad for Peggy. When we're in our room at night I try and ask her stuff, but she never tells me anything about how she feels or if something is bothering her. I've gotten used to her being like that, but I feel so depressed. Especially when Mom screams in frustration at her, I know Peggy must feel awful. I rock back and forth for hours feeling sad and don't know what is the matter. Maybe she has cancer.

Last week, six months since I wrote the above, they took Peggy to the mental hospital. That day she got up and started out for church. She said there was to be a special service just for her and the whole parish would be there. She yelled at Mom and Dad to hurry up and get dressed. Then she started praying on her knees in the kitchen. They think she has schizophrenia.

Knowing the name doesn't comfort me but it dispels some of the fear that grows in ignorance. As Dorothy Thompson once said, "Fear grows in darkness. If you think there's a bogeyman around, turn on the light." Naming the illness is a light, and the first step toward seeking relief for my sister's pain, and my own grief, too. I'm thankful for that.

"To everyone, his own life is a mystery."

The weariness in her voice was palpable over the thousand miles that separated us. Theresa suffered with schizophrenia twenty years. Then just when her symptoms were in remission, she developed breast cancer. Despite a mastectomy, it had metastasized and she dreaded the chemotherapy.

"I decided to have no more of the chemotherapy, Jane. It makes me feel so sick. It's been one thing after another. Why has God done this? - I have suffered so much. I don't know, I just don't know what my life is all about," her voice trailed off, bewildered.

I murmured words of hope and comfort as best I could. I told her we would visit soon, that the kids would write, to keep up her beautiful knitting. After all, she was only 43. Her Good-bye had a desperate finality to it. The next morning when it was time for discharge, she was found dead in the shower.

Like her life, her death was a mystery. I think she was saying, "God, why have you forsaken me?" And He heard.

Death may be the final deliverance from pain and suffering. But deliverance can also come from release of our demands, changing our attitudes, giving up having to know or having to control. Deliverance comes with surrender to the mysteries of life.

"Pain is life - the sharper, the more evidence of life."
Charles Lamb

My life will never be the same since that stunning day Peter went totally crazy. We were getting ready to go to the grocery store when he suddenly announced he was catching a train to Washington, D.C. He had a special mission to tell the president about a secret plot the Iranians had to take over the whole city. I still can hear his raving and threats when we wouldn't let him go. Everybody in the neighborhood must have heard us. I can't face them, or my boss, or anybody. I can't bear it. We've been good parents, done what's right, have a standing in the community, getting ready to retire. Now this. We always thought he was just a little retarded when he couldn't do the school work and had no friends. But CRAZY?! NO! Not full of strange voices telling him his sister is the secret head of the F.B.I. There are times I wish...I wish God would take him. It sounds awful, but I think death would be better than this. How can I wish my own child dead?

Maybe I am so angry because I think I am special. I shouldn't have sorrows and burdens. Why not? I'm no different from other people. My afflictions make me part of the human race. To be alive is to feel pain. I can forge my anger into strength.

"A man can have one death, one life; one heaven, one hell. I count life just as stuff to try the soul's strength on."
Robert Browning

"The weight of this sad time we must obey:
Speak what we feel, not what we ought to say."
Wm. Shakespeare

Maybe I ought to say "I accept this; I can handle this." But the truth is I feel enormously jealous of people who are healthy and have healthy families. I feel jealous even of people who have physical illness. Even though mental illnesses are as physically based as any other, they are not generally accepted on a par. Those with other disorders do not bear the stigma that mental illness imposes on all of us associated with it. Physical ailments evoke empathy; mental ailments evoke fear and fear engenders cruelty. What other illness makes you turn yourself inside out to keep it secret? What other illness is associated in peoples' minds with convicts, prostitutes, and drug addicts? I envy the smug wellness, the freedom from stigma, the self assuredness of the healthy and the physically ill.

No wonder there are some who believe the emotion of envy is biologically rooted in us. It seems to be a universal feeling. The very first referral to "sin" mentioned in the Bible is not Eve and the apple, but Cain's jealousy of Abel. My feelings of jealousy and envy are part of the human condition. So, I voice them, knowing they are part of "the weight of this sad time."

"I knew a witty physician who found religious creed in the biliary duct and used to affirm that if there was a disease in the liver the man became a Calvinist."

R. W. Emerson

You can't imagine the relief it was to me to realize that religious beliefs could be influenced by physical and mental deficiencies, and they did not necessarily reflect God's teachings. My father was a minister whose religion tyrannized me. For years I felt as though this enormous eagle hovered over me questioning and judging my every move. When I look back now, I can see how paranoid and distorted his interpretations were. But I also realize how sick and depressed a person he was and how this colored his religion. His God of wrath and destruction sprang from his troubled mind.

"God moves in a mysterious way
His wonders to perform."
Wm. Cowper

*"There is no greater grief than to remember days
of gladness when sorrow is at hand."*
Friedrich Schiller

My daughter is diagnosed schizophrenic. The hardest part is giving up all the dreams of a husband, career, or a normal life for her. I look in her room at her drawings and think of the artist she may have been. I weep at the photos of her in a prom gown, at the beach, as a little girl riding a pony. How can I reconcile that carefree happy face with the unpredictable stranger I see now? I ache for those days past; my heart cries out, "Come back, come back. This present is a dreadful mistake."

It is taking a long time for me to accept another kind of life for her. She may not be a great artist; she'll most likely not marry and I won't have grandchildren. Things are irrevocably different and I must learn other joys and goals. The pleasures of the past sting if I cling to them.

*"Grief is the agony of a minute. The indulgence
of grief is the blunder of a life."*
B. Disraeli

*"There is a sort of knowledge that only
experience can give."*

When my older brother, Tom, was admitted to the psychiatric
unit, I would not go to see him. Tom was bright, good looking,
someone I looked up to and hoped to emulate. He had graduated
from the state's finest university, and I had recently been accepted
there. I had a friend who got depressed and was treated by a
psychiatrist. He got better and life went on. I thought it would be
so with Tom. My folks kept begging me to accompany them.
They told me he would be in the hospital a long time. But I could
not accept the fact that there was anything seriously wrong.
Finally, I visited during the Christmas holidays. Tom had put on
twenty pounds; his hair was shaggy and oily. We talked about
football, school, and the weather. Sometimes he stared off into
space. I felt creepy. Then he drew me close and his eyes bore
into me. "You must get me out of here, Jimmy. Dr. Miller is
going to kill me. The voices tell me it will be soon."

It was then I realized that Tom was terribly, truly, terrifyingly
sick. And like a poison rising up in my gut and threading through
my brain, seeped the thought, "Could this happen to me?"

**It is hard to convey in words what it is like to have someone
close succumb to a major mental illness. Books may describe,
people can tell you, but there is a hidden core of meaning that
only the experience of it gives. Isn't this true of a great deal in
life? Like an exquisite melody, or the fragrance of a rose, or the
void of a loss, this kind of knowledge pierces the heart and soul.
It is a lesson written not in texts, but in the book of life.**

*"Knowledge is proud that he has learned so much.
Wisdom is humble that he knows no more."*
Wm. Cowper

Charlie came to me depressed and in chronic pain after several unsuccessful back surgeries. I taught him to use biofeedback for pain control and put him on a regimen of antidepressants. Both helped him greatly. Although unable to work outside his home, he kept busy weaving rugs and wood carving. I didn't hear from him for a year.

Then, one day quite by accident, I heard Charlie had locked himself in the garage, in his car, and let the motor run. I felt ice in the pit of my stomach and weak with sadness. "Charlie, why didn't you call? I could have helped you. Why?" Impotence became me badly for I was accustomed to taking charge, doing things and having answers.

How often have we said "I should have done something," "I ought to have known," "This shouldn't have happened." But events sometimes unfold regardless of us and oblivious to our knowledge or abilities to intervene. Such times confront our pride and self-assuredness. Such times teach us humility, an essential ingredient of wisdom.

"Everyone has his secret sorrows which the world knows not."
H. W. Longfellow

I never told anyone in school about my mom. She called my sister and me sluts and yelled in our faces at us for no reason. She was a fanatic about things being dirty and went around taking every little spot off the windows. If we left books on the table, she would throw them in the trash. She was suspicious of Dad's mail and would open the letters to see what he was hiding from her. One day she threw a frying pan at him. He would threaten to divorce her to make her take her medication. Whenever we were asked if our mothers would volunteer for school events, I always said she was too busy or she was ill. With my friends I acted all smiles and happy. I looked like "Miss Perfect," but I wept in my heart.

"As one whom the mother caresses, so will I comfort you."
Isaiah 66:13

Sometimes God is the only One who knows our misery. I go where I can be quiet and silent and know that She knows. I do not even have to say a word.

16

Mary Heaney

"Coldly, sadly descends the Autumn evening. The field strewn with dank yellow drifts of withered leaves."
Matthew Arnold, Rugby Chapel

Winter is doubly bleak and chilly, due to my wife's Seasonal Affective Disorder. For months we have practically no social life. She is grumpy and sad, gorges on sweets and lies around half the morning. Our sex life is nonexistent. I make excuses with our friends and try everything to cheer her. Then, with Spring, it's like a butterfly emerging from a cocoon. She flits all over the place getting involved with all sorts of activities. She gets irritable and argumentative if I can't or won't keep up with her enormous energy level. After all I did to get her through the winter, she isn't even grateful, nor does she seem to remember how down she was. Her illness has kept our marriage on a see-saw, although with light therapy and antidepressants, things are improving.

"Melancholy is the nurse of frenzy."
Shakespeare

We tend to think of mental illness as a static thing, but Seasonal Affective Disorder reminds us that mental disorders can and do vary considerably. No mood remains unaltered over time. If we recognize in someone early deterioration, or signs of a change in mood and symptoms, we can often help to check a full blown relapse.

"God loves an idle rainbow
No less than laboring seas."
                                    R. Hedgson

My best friend dropped out of college last year. He is so bright he could be an engineer or a scientist, and he has artistic talent too. Now, since he had a psychotic breakdown, he doesn't even talk about school. The doctors are going to try one of the newer antipsychotic drugs. He likes to help me tinker with my car, but most of the time he sits around worrying. He is starting to paint water colors though. His father says, "I guess he'll never amount to anything now that this has happened." What does that mean, "amount to anything"? It sounds like a verdict of worthlessness.

We measure the worth of people by what they can do. We tend to think in terms of sick or well, all or nothing, success or failure. But there are countless variations and degrees of life and as many ways to live as there are people. There is no such thing as "never amounting to anything". Whose life is perfect? Whose life is pointless?

WAYS TO COPE

"HE WHO SINGS FRIGHTENS AWAY ILLS."

CERVANTES

"When I hear music I fear no danger...
I am invulnerable, I see no foe."
H. D. Thoreau

Did you know that a set of headphones and cassette player can ease away the intruding voices of psychosis? A social worker told me this. She observed the number of mentally ill patients, the younger ones especially, who love to listen to their Walkmans. It seems the music distracts their auditory hallucinations. Of course there are some who wonder if it isn't modern maniacal rock music that causes psychosis!

Nevertheless, music goes where words cannot. Music reaches the depths of a person and speaks the language of emotions. In biblical times, music was known to "soothe the savage beast." It bridges the gap between emotions and words.

Enjoy music frequently to relieve stress, provide respite from cares. To enrich your daily life, take a music break.

"Music exalts each joy, allays each grief
Expels diseases, softens pain
Subdues rages of passion."
John Armstrong, 1744

Mary Heaney

"All griefs with bread are less."
George Herbert, <u>Proverbs</u>

I call it **"pie therapy"** because the first time I experienced it was over a piece of lemon meringue pie with my best friend. It could be called "coffee therapy" or "popcorn therapy" just as well. To sit and share food with a trusted friend is balm to troubled spirits. My lemon meringue pie friend moved several hundred miles away. Even so, when I am particularly distressed, I call and she responds, "Is it pie therapy time?"

I know another woman who cares for her elderly, mentally ill father. Her sixteen year old next door neighbor comes in every day after school and shares a pot of "tea therapy". It's the high point of their day.

Probably the oldest and most human solace is the breaking of bread together. It's a symbol of compassion, concern, friendship. This simple pleasure eases life's burdens. Use "pie therapy" regularly.

"A man needs a little madness, or else he will never cut the rope and be free."

Zorba the Greek

One way to look at mental illness in my family is as a catalyst to change. Consider the shame and stigma I feel by association. If I agree with society's judgements, I acquiesce in my own bondage. If I cannot accept my own relatedness to "madness", how can I accept the "other" who is mentally ill? The illness becomes a powerful stimulus to unqualified acceptance. If I cast off the social shackles of prejudice, if **I do not care about them**, I am free. I have "cut the rope". What a relief it is, for the most devastating thing about mental illness is not the illness but the stigma attached to it. Freeing myself of bondage to the stigma, I change my attitude and that makes all the difference. I choose freedom!

"Thus you free yourself from bondage, from both good and evil karma; through your non-attachment, you embody me, in utter freedom."

The Bhagavad Gita

"Too much sanity may be madness."
Don Quixote

My sister, Jane, and I took our cousin, Lois, on an outing from the state hospital. Lois burst into the restaurant grinning from ear to ear. She wore a hopelessly outmoded red floral print dress, white socks with black patent leather shoes, and several neon colored barrettes in her hair. Embarrassed, Jane quickly shuttled her to a dim corner table. "Oh, look at the pretty flowers," Lois blared delightedly to the vase on the table. Although thirty, her voice mimicked a ten year old. "Shush, quiet," pleaded Jane. On it went: Lois, naive, inept, and bizarre, was having a perfectly marvelous time. Jane, uptight, awkward, trying to be proper, spent a miserable afternoon.

Sometimes it is best to lower expectations in order to enjoy the moment. Insisting on the planned, the rational and the "correct" can spoil having fun together. If we feel embarrassed by our loved one's bizarre behavior, enjoy time together in private places. To never deviate from the clock and the rules may be as crazy as not knowing what the rules are.

I will remember, in the words of Don Quixote, to sometimes "lay down the melancholy burden of sanity." My mentally ill friend reminds me to lighten up and not take rules and regulations and social constrictions too seriously. To appear a bit odd isn't the end of the world!

"He who plays the piano keeps sane."
Italian Proverb

How do you keep your **own** sanity? One of the best ways is to have an absorbing hobby or interest. It may be music, gardening, collecting thimbles, a sport, studying English history, arranging flowers, or knitting, but it must interest you. Taking a little time every day to concentrate on this activity tranquilizes the mind and centers the spirit. It provides a focal point for emotional and intellectual activity. It is as necessary as food or sleep.

A retired gentleman enjoyed playing his guitar and kept urging his wife, who suffered recurring depression, to try painting again. As a young woman, she had dabbled in art. Finally he bought her some water colors. Not only did the painting ease her depression, she was **good** at it! Her pictures appeared in exhibits and she acquired a network of fellow artists. What's good for the well is good for the sick!

Wake each day anticipating your "special time." Let the joy of your hobby be a focal point for the day. There is no better way to help others than to be happy yourself.

*"Never argue with a crazy person, because
you'll never win."*
                                        Irish Proverb

When Dad's paranoid schizophrenia would get worse, I would
just go to my room and listen to music or study. You'd have to let
him go on and on. I mean, if you said, "No, those pictures on the
wall are not talking to you; or that lady next door isn't spying on
you," he would just get louder and more vehement. But my sister,
Anna, would not ignore his delusions. She kept thinking he
WOULD change his ideas if she argued enough. No matter how
outrageous Dad's ideas, she would logically and loudly point out
their absurdity. Of course he just became noisier and more
insistent. At last she has learned to stay calm and has given up
trying to win useless arguments.

**Learning what to ignore saves us frustration and grief. Don't
argue with delusions; accept peculiar preferences or distastes.
It is a skill to distinguish between what is annoying and incon-
venient or embarrassing from what is unsafe, dangerous or un-
acceptable.**

*"A wise man sees as much as he ought, not as
much as he can."*
                                        Michel de Montaigne

"When helpers fail and comforts flee, I find help from I know not where."

M. Gandhi

William Cowper, born in Berkhamsted, England, loved writing poetry. But his father, a clergyman, insisted his son study law. Caught between the two pursuits, William plunged into a deep depression.

Hospitalized for his deteriorating condition, he happened to read the story of Jesus raising Lazarus from the dead, and that helped him recover. After his release, he joined with John Newton, a minister, in publishing the "Olney Hymns" in 1779. His best known is "God Moves in a Mysterious Way."

"O Lord! My best desires fulfill. And help me resign Life, health, and comfort to Thy will. Make thy pleasure mine."

William Cowper

"We're all prisoners, Chicky Baby!"

This line, from a movie whose title I do not even remember, is a standing joke with my husband and me. In one of life's darkest moments, it brought laughter, and has become a symbol of hope and humor. Whenever either of us feels especially down, we say, "we're ALL prisoners, Chicky Baby." This was the first movie we had seen since our son had a psychotic breakdown. He was living at home, and we felt imprisoned by the circumscribed life we now led because of his illness. In the movie, a fellow was alluding to another character who was thought to be "mental" and a prisoner of his distorted mind. They were being served at a fast food joint, and the waitress rolled her eyes and remarked, "We're ALL prisoners, Chicky Baby." We laughed like a dam overflowing and all the pent up emotional tension was released.

We are all prisoners: prisoners of prejudice, the past, our irrational thoughts and expectations. As long as these hold us captive, we can not appreciate the moment of laughter that may grace the present.

> *"With the fearful strains upon me, if I did not laugh, I would die."*
> **Abraham Lincoln**

"There are two ways to get enough. One is to accumulate more and more. The other is to want less."

G.K. Chesterton

Our society prides itself on accomplishments, striving, becoming better and better, and getting more and more. This represents "the good life". Demands on individuals are great, resulting in high levels of stress and expectations, with proportional prejudice on those who cannot measure up. This may be why the mentally ill are so stigmatized in our society compared to other less exacting cultures. Some studies show that where tolerance of mentally ill people is higher, less blame is put upon them and their families. The actual severity of the illness may even be less in cultures other than highly industrialized, achievement-oriented societies. Our society's huge expectation of how people "should be" sets the stage for severe stigma and discrimination.

The higher our expectations, the more we set ourselves up for disappointments. It is in demanding less that we feel a sense of abundance. Let tolerance begin with ourselves. Let us learn to not judge ourselves harshly, nor to afflict ourselves with pressure and hurrying all the time.

Take a deep breath and be open to the present moment without expectation. Then, the joy we find in simple words and gestures may spread to others so they too may become tolerant.

"I have learned in whatsoever state I am, to be content."
Philippians IV 11:60

"The only cure for grief is action."
G. H. Lewes

No day passes without some sorrow, especially when we are daily confronted with the disordered, confused, distressing reality of mental illness. It helps to become involved in groups and activities devoted to sharing, and support such as the National Alliance for the Mentally Ill and its local organizations. Become active in these groups and study all you can. I know one woman who published a booklet of available mental health services in her community. Another man and his wife are politically active in the advocacy movement. A computer user started an electronic bulletin board support group in his area. Still another organized social outings for her son and a small group of other friends with mental illnesses.

The important thing to remember is to engage yourself in relevant action.

"The more you grieve, the greater is your loss."
Persian Proverb

Therefore, I will waste little time quarreling with my daily sorrow but take up the burden in some positive action.

"Does God exact day labor, light denied ?"
John Milton

The answer is, "Of course not." The poet Milton wrote these anguished words when he became blind. God does not expect the impossible. So often we demand of ourselves more than is realistically possible.

My friend agonized over keeping her son at home, despite her fears and the fact that his medication needed continual readjustments. After she found him wandering around the house one night with a knife, she knew that she was inadequate to the task. A year later, she was able to have him home again, profoundly improved. A "light" in the form of new medication vastly improved his symptoms where other antipsychotics had failed.

If we are expected to do something, the means will present themselves. Likewise, if we are attempting the impossible, perhaps we are ignoring important signs, clues, or advice. If God does not expect day labor light denied, why should we?

*"A moment's insight is sometimes worth
a life's experience."*
                                    O. W. Holmes

The kids and I kept hoping that Harry would realize the impact of his hypomanic behavior on us. We thought if he only had insight into how his irritability, control, and overbearing intrusiveness affected our relationships, he would somehow change. Telling him later when his mood was normal seemed to have little effect. For a long time we stubbornly clung to the fantasy that one day he would say, "God, my behavior is awful - it must hurt you, and I am so sorry." That was a delusion! Once we got rid of this expectation, we could deal with him in a common-sense way. After years of frustrating experience, and wasted effort, I was the one to gain insight!

Manics are notoriously, maddeningly, lacking in insight. Then, in their normal states, they can't seem to reconstruct their behavior reliably. They are difficult people to be around. As one doctor put it, "Depressives are hard on themselves; manics on everyone else around them."

Life becomes easier when we let go of demands, expectations, and not permit them to get the best of us. It is folly to hold a person and a relationship hostage for years, waiting for them to "gain insight". It's more productive for US to get the insight and act accordingly in our own self interest!

"Too long a sacrifice makes a stone of the heart."
W. B. Yeats, Easter, 1916

After her first breakdown, my parents' life revolved around my schizophrenic sister. They spent all their time with her, tried to be everything for her: socially, emotionally, vocationally. They put their own lives and interests aside; they could not enjoy a balanced life during retirement years. Peggy did not seem to improve all that much after several years. It was apparent that her prognosis was not bright and her condition, though stabilized, would be chronic. Then a sad thing happened. They ignored her. It was as if they had exhausted themselves to the point where they were depleted of good will. Eventually, when Peggy relapsed and had to be committed to the hospital, they sighed with relief. They did not visit; they did not even send her a birthday card. I felt so bad that I signed their names and wrote a note from them on a card because Peggy asked about them.

Depriving myself does not help my sick relative. If I care for myself and my needs, I can better care for others. A healthy balance is the key.

"In moderation there is stability."
Seneca

"Every new adjustment is a crisis in self esteem."
Eric Hoffer

In the two years since my daughter was diagnosed schizophrenic, it has been constant turmoil for me - just one thing after another to try to get used to. Every turn and symptom of her illness mocks my confidence and coping ability. She bathes once a week, and then only when I insist. She scowls at friends when they visit so I have cut back on visitors. Sometimes she walks outdoors half undressed and I must put up with people complaining that she digs in their trash. I sometimes feel ashamed, resentful, exasperated, like a prisoner in my own home. The other family members all are affected by the social stigma and by these blows to our self esteem. Every day it's like the gauntlet is thrown down, "Can you cope?"

"Two in distress make sorrow less."
H. G. Bohn, <u>Handbook of Proverbs</u>

When I feel like a prisoner, I know it's time to seek out a friend from our local support group. Knowing there is someone else who shares these problems eases the burden. A telephone call, an hour out shopping or having coffee is not a luxury; it is a necessity.

"If it were not for hope, the heart would break."
English Proverb

The researcher needs confidence that a better drug is indeed possible. Clinicians must trust new treatments and rely on biological processes. Loved ones hope for, if not cures, at least easing of symptoms. A woman grasped at every new drug for her schizophrenic son. He had been at times on Thorazine, Haldol, and Stelazine. Improvement was minimal and his frequent admissions to the hospital came as a relief because he endangered himself by living on the street. A new medication turned out to be a miracle. He now works part time and has a girlfriend. His mother is overwhelmed with joy. But she realizes that her hope all those years had made each day bearable. That was the value of hope; even if there had not been a breakthrough in his treatment, it sustained the present. It kept her heart from breaking, regardless of any future outcome.

"To travel hopefully is a better thing than to arrive."
R. L. Stevenson

Hope, a trust that situations will improve, that the future may hold promise, is not pie-in-the sky, Pollyanna idleness. It is a surrender to the positive forces working the world. Cultivate an attitude of hope, for without it life is more than bleak: it's heartbreaking.

"Children have long ears and quick tongues."
                                    Bohn's <u>Book of Proverbs</u>

My brother was having one of his paranoid spells and was especially agitated because our cousin, whom he disliked, had stopped
by with her five year old daughter. Although he has never hit me,
he started to scream angrily at me. The little girl happened to
come into the living room just then and she said to me with all the
authority of a grown woman, "If he tries to hit you, scream for
murder, Aunt Marie." That got me laughing and broke the tension
enough, so I walked out with her and left Jay alone for a while.

**Sometimes we let our mentally ill relative "get away with mur-
der" because we mistakenly feel that since he is sick, we should
not demand anything from him. Setting limits on disruptive
behavior, adhering to some schedule, keeping structure in our
environment is actually helpful to a disorganized person. Al-
lowing time out alone is a good way to stop a disturbing situation before it gets out of hand. Like Greta Garbo, sometimes it
is good to say, "I want to be alone."**

*"It is not our differences that really matter. It is
the meanness behind that is ugly."*
M. Gandhi

Each person must determine how much time he can spend with
someone who is mentally ill without losing his own equanimity.
My sister criticizes me repeatedly for not spending more time
with our brother. She is a nurse and maybe that is why she
tolerates him so admirably. The truth is, I feel unnerved and
depressed after more than a couple of hours once a week. We
spend a few hours at lunch or a movie or shopping and that's it.
Besides, I figure if I get upset, how does that help the sick person?
I try to explain this but my sister interprets differences as selfish-
ness, which makes her angry.

"We are all crazy when we are angry," the ancient Philemon
**reminds us. It is especially crazy to stir up strife by family mem-
bers accusing and berating each other over how and when to
help their sick member. There will be differences and each must
do what he is best suited to.**

"Often the test of courage is not to die but to live."
Vittorio Alfieri

When I lost my job, I put my head down on the desk, devastated.
I felt completely useless, because my wife and a mentally ill
adolescent son were dependent on my income. What seemed
even worse, was the thought of not practicing my profession. For
a year I got one rejection after the other. I remember lying on the
sofa thinking it would be better for them if I were dead and they'd
have my life insurance. My wife was asking me to take a walk
with her. I kept thinking, "Wouldn't it be brave and man-like to
just grab the gun?" Somehow at that moment it seemed to take
far more guts to get up and take a walk than to sink into oblivion.
I just lay there for a while and gradually I found the strength to
drag myself off that sofa and go for a walk.

**They say courage may be taught just as a child learns to speak.
It helps to have early examples of courage. But if we remain
still and listen, we may find a place of courage deep within waiting to be tapped. Instead of rushing to always do something,
take a few minutes each day to be quiet, still. By refraining from
action, we touch our inner feelings, we allow things to resolve.
We may find the courage to go on.**

"In mental illness the capacity to relax is as much impaired as the integrity of a bone is destroyed by fractures."

Abraham Myerson

Aunt Helen suffered severe anxiety and panic attacks. Once I was driving with her and she came to a bridge. She started gasping for breath and trembling. She pulled over and had me drive over the bridge, and after that she was afraid to drive anywhere. When she had the attacks, my uncle Mike would keep telling her, "Now, Helen, take a deep breath, JUST RELAX!!!" This was the very thing she could **not** do.

In obsessive-compulsive disorder, washing a hundred times is still never enough to dispel the anxiety. In depression, negative thoughts torment endlessly. In mania, the pressure to talk is like a speeding locomotive. The schizophrenic mind is in a continual state of tension. It's striking how the inability to relax underlies the whole spectrum of mental illness, causing so much anguish.

It may have been better had Uncle Mike taken her for a brisk walk. After all, physical activity is one of the surest antidotes to anxiety for everyone.

I remind myself to exercise in some way every day. By safeguarding my own ability to relax, I enhance those around me. As surely as the bone mends by immobilization; my mind mends in physical mobility.

"The Truth shall make you free."
                              Gospel of St. John, 32

It happened when I was six, but I never knew my uncle committed suicide until I was 50 years old. No one in our family mentioned this secret during all those years. Some people say these
things are better **not** known. What difference does it make? To
me, however, knowing it explained things I never understood, like
why Dad never took me to his brother's home or talked about
him. Why Dad himself seemed depressed a lot of the time and
why he had an irrational fear of one of his friends committing
suicide. I wonder if Dad or I will ever think of suicide, or my
son? Knowing we have depressive tendencies that are treatable
makes me freer than my uncle was.

**To know the truth about one's family is to be prepared. Know-
ing my vulnerabilities makes me afraid sometimes, but it is "that
peculiar kind of fear they call courage." It is the courage to know
the truth and seek solutions. Ignorance only compounds problems.**

"Truth unites; Falsehood divides."
A. Einstein

His mother said it was because I smoked when I was pregnant. My mom said Harry was too harsh on Joel. I said we should have sent him to a private school. Harry insisted Joel wanted to be babied all his life. My sister said his lousy diet was the cause. We tortured and blamed ourselves trying to find reasons why this happened.

In the Bible they asked Jesus of the blind young man, "Is it because of the sins of the parents?" The insinuation was that when misfortune strikes, "we have it coming to us". People become mentally ill because their faith isn't strong enough, or they have not lived righteous lives, or their upbringing is faulty.

When our son had a psychotic episode our whole family went to pieces for a while. We were torn apart by guilt and blame. Now we know our son has a serious illness that requires lifelong treatment. That's the truth that unites us.

When mental illness appears we frantically focus on "Why did it happen?" instead of "How can I help?" How useless are recriminations and accusations. We know there are many genetic and environmental antecedents to schizophrenia and other mental illnesses. By finding out the truth about the disease, by separating the falsehoods, by refusing to blame, we are powerful champions of unity.

*"There is a weird power in the spoken word, and
a word carries far and deals destruction through
time as bullets flying through space."*
                                        J. Conrad

"I know Jim doesn't hate me when he goes on tirades. The words tumble from a distorted and tortured mind. It's easy when the words are obviously untrue, but sometimes they take me by surprise. They strike so sharply personal and he looks at me so intensely, I can't help feeling hurt."

The "weird power of the spoken word" is not an easy thing to shake off. We associate language with meaning and intent. But in many cases of emotional disturbance words are more like random electrical particles. Just because they may be in sequence doesn't mean they have meaning. They may only be focal points for deranged neurotransmitters.

When crazy words get to me, I go where there is quiet. My favorite place is a park nearby where there is a path along the river. Someone once said, "There is no misery an hour's walk will not soothe." Sometimes I call or visit a friend. When I take care of my own mental equilibrium, I realize words can be "full of sound and fury, signifying nothing".

"Oh that pang where more than madness lies;
the worm that will not sleep nor die."
Lord Byron

The pang, the worm that Lord Byron, the poet, speaks of is guilt. It wasn't so long ago that parents, mothers especially, were considered to be the cause of their child's mental illness. Mental Health professionals endlessly unraveled every event, every nuance of interaction, analyzing and interpreting. From time immemorial, the worm of guilt has devoured mothers when something bad happens to their child. It is as spontaneous and pervasive as tears. The trouble with looking for causes is that our attention is diverted away from solutions. We become so mired in guilt that we are glued to it, unable to effectively pursue the present moment. Even if guilt were justified because of some lapse on our part, correction comes not from wallowing in guilt, but persevering with courage in our present duties. Learning and studying about a loved one's illness enables us to see how multi-faceted the illness is and how much is yet unknown. His own resilience, biology, and the environment all have an impact.

The support and help I offer now, no matter how much or how little, can influence the course of the disease. Harboring guilt about the past is not only unreasonable, it is crippling.

"The firmest friendships have been formed in mutual adversity."

Charles Colton

My mom kept telling me to include Eleanor, who was a year older, in my social life. Her eccentric ways embarrassed me. My friends were tolerant enough but I could not overcome my shame. A lot of times I made up excuses not to include her, and then I'd feel guilty. A girl I did not know well started to hang around with us and she told me about her younger brother who had mental problems and was so difficult to live with. Here was someone who understood! It changed my world. We became such good friends that she could tell my sister things like, "You're a good egg, even though you're a little cracked." Then we would all laugh.

You can't pick your relatives, but thank goodness for friends! People who have a problem similar to mine have become my best friends. Support groups like my local branch of the Alliance for the Mentally Ill are a lifeline to me.

God gives us bewildering relatives, but we can choose understanding friends.

WHAT THE ILL CONTRIBUTE AND TEACH US

"I HAVE NEVER MET A MAN SO IGNORANT
I COULD NOT LEARN SOMETHING FROM
HIM."

GALILEO

"AND GLADLY WOULD I LEARN, AND
GLADLY TEACH."

CHAUCER,
<u>CANTERBURY</u> <u>TALES</u>

"Insanity destroys reason, but not wit."
Nathaniel Emmons

In her manic times, Grandma kept us exhausted, and sometimes laughing, with her non-stop talk, witticisms, racing here and there, making jokes and puns. When she went into a severe depression, the doctor recommended electro-shock treatment. That worried me because I had heard stories about people turning into zombies and losing their memory after shock treatment. After the first one, I visited her and she did seem dopey. After a few more, when I went to see her, she waved at me and declared, "Well, honey, they plugged me into Northern States Power and my light came back on." We had our grandma back again!

Some of the world's cleverest poetry has been written by artists suffering from manic-depressive illness. Many writers and comedians suffer dark nights of depression. Our loved ones appreciate a good joke and a funny movie as much as anyone. Maybe more. Sickness doesn't mean somber.

*"What harm is there in getting knowledge and
learning, were it from a sot, a pot, a fool, a winter
mitten, or an old slipper?"*

Rabelais

Jack was a tall, emaciated silent young man of thirty who lived
next door to us and everyone said was "queer". On summer
evenings I watched intrigued as he strolled his yard staring at the
stars and muttering to himself. There was a brick alleyway
separating our houses and a wrought iron fence overgrown with
lilacs. He didn't work; his sister took care of him. I pretended to
pick lilacs and watched him puttering around on his porch. He
made my mother very nervous and I heard the word "mental"
whispered about him. One July afternoon, however, I found the
nerve to say "Hello." After that we acknowledged each other and
eventually talked over the fence. He told me all about the constel-
lations, the phases of the moon, tales of meteors and comets. To
my twelve year old mind, Jack was an encyclopedia of astronomy.
Everything I know about the heavens to this day I learned from
"queer Jack". I can't look at the milky way without thinking of
him.

**We learn in the most unlikely of places and from the simplest of
people. Everyone has something to teach if we are receptive.
The key to being receptive is giving up prejudice. As one wit put
it, "Minds are like parachutes. They only work when they are
open."**

*"Lack of something to feel important about is
almost the greatest tragedy a person may have."*
Arthur E. Morgan

Our daughter's psychosis centered around religious themes. At
first, we regretted that we had stressed religion so much in our
family, mistakenly thinking that this caused Amber's illness.
Later, after she became stabilized on medication, her religion and
spiritual values found a relevant and legitimate place.

Amber became the "prayer person" of our large family. She was
a natural, with much empty time to fill, while we all hurried
through our days of work, families, and an excess of activities.
Whenever someone felt the strain of an unsolved problem, an
illness, a sorrow or a joy, it was Amber we called upon to inter-
cede with her prayers. "Dan takes his exam tomorrow, Amber,
don't forget." "I'm so worried about Sally, please pray for her."
"Paul and John aren't getting along at all, remember them,
Amber." She had a steady stream of requests and fulfilled her
role proudly. It was comforting to know someone "prayed
unceasingly" for our needs.

"All service is the same with God."
Robert Browning

"No man is so rich that he does not need another's help; no man is so poor as to be not useful in some way......to ask assistance and to grant it are part of our very nature."
Pope Leo XII

Audrey heard voices and refused to go into rooms painted pink. But her chocolate cake was a marvel. She cooked delicious meals for her aging parents and, although she needed transportation, did most of the grocery shopping. Her day centered around planning the evening meal, which she did with as much enthusiasm and pride as Julia Childs.

In a survey of 725 clients and their families in Wisconsin, sixty percent contributed to their household in some way. Most of them had been diagnosed at about age 21 and had been ill an average of 17 years. *(Journal of Hospital and Community Psychiatry, May, 1994.)* They provided companionship and helped with many chores such as cleaning, shopping, cooking, and providing news of other family members. Acknowledging these contributions help counter the negative self esteem people with mental illness have and enhances their image in the community. Families who participated in the survey were anxious to share these positive contributions the clients made and felt it was therapeutic to recognize them. Reporting these may help reduce the stigma associated with mental illness.

When it comes to household participation, it helps to strike a balance. We must guard against having such low expectations that we give no opportunity for helping. On the other hand, expecting too much can disappoint if the job done does not measure up to our standards.

"You can't be brave if you've had only wonderful things happen to you."

Mary Tyler Moore

My dad's bouts of hostile hypomania would lay me low. I'd mope around unable to do anything, feeling both dejected and angry. Looking back I realize I was depressed a lot of the time. One day, I just ran out the door and I ran and ran with tears streaming down my face. I kept thinking maybe there was a reason God was letting this happen to me. But then I'd think that was crazy – maybe I should just move out. Why would God want me to be a martyr? Especially if feeling victimized sapped all my energy. After an hour, I felt better; at least I couldn't cry any more.

About that time, the track season was starting at school and I went out for the longer distances. On training runs, all kinds of thoughts surfaced. I'd feel lousy over Dad's latest storm. Then I'd think, well, maybe I'm supposed to learn how to deal with all this and stop feeling sorry for myself. One thing was certain – the more I ran, the better I felt. By the time track season ended, I felt strong enough to seek counselling, which helped me sort things out. I think going through that bad time has given me courage and self reliance.

"Strength is born in the deep silence of long-suffering hearts, not amidst joy."

Felicia Dorothea Browne Hemans

A bout of depression can be a catalyst to change, a challenge to self knowledge, makes one stronger and more resilient. Psychiatrist Frederic Flach believes this often is the case. He describes this in his book, <u>The Secret Strength of Depression.</u>

"To catch the golden moment of opportunity and the good within our reach, that is the great art of life."
Samuel Johnson

Peggy's sister, Jean, had schizophrenia. Peggy had mixed feelings about her. On the one hand, she felt sorry for her sister; yet she resented the fact that their mother expected her to include Jean in her activities.

One day they went to a nearby amusement park with a group of Peggy's friends. Mother had warned them about wild, scary rides, particularly the roller coasters and the ferris wheel. Peggy very cautiously took Jean on only the mildest amusements. Then they walked past the ferris wheel. "Let's go on it," cried Jean. She promptly went up to the ticket taker and soon was ensconced on the next swaying seat. Peggy froze in terror. Not only the fear of disobeying Mom, but her own fear of heights paralyzed her. She could not bring herself to get on, even as Jean pleaded and the ticket taker held the seat still and patiently waited.

At last she shook her head and mumbled, "I'll watch." Round and round went the ferris wheel to Jean's laughter and Peggy's chagrin. Concepts of who is fragile and who is strong crumbled as she watched stunned. How could her frail, nervous, medicated sibling who needed protection do such an outrageous thing as ride the ferris wheel in carefree abandon? They never told Mother, of course. But from that day there was a hint of admiration in Peggy and a glow of pride in Jean for "catching the golden moment".

It may be a good thing to feel "inferior" sometimes, especially when compared to someone about whom you have felt "superior". It puts things in perspective. We learn the awful truth that everyone is inferior in some way and everyone is superior in some way, and these perceptions can dissolve in the spin of a ferris wheel!

*"Adversity elicits talents which otherwise would
have lain dormant."*
                                                    Horace

I've been what they call a "spinster" all these years. I'm used to
things arranged just so, with white doilies on my tables and knick
knacks dusted every Saturday. When my niece was left homeless,
I took her in to live with me. My knowledge of her mental
problems had been limited to weekly visits. At first I was unnerved by her crying bouts, silly laughter at nothing, her hours of
religious devotions and rambling conversations. Each day
exhausted me and I think if there had been another relative to do
the job I would have given up in exasperation.

With lots of reading, and going to a support group I have learned
a great deal about medication, and how to interact with someone
whose thinking is confused. It has not been easy, yet I feel proud
of my new skills and abilities. For someone who has lived alone,
it is like handling a family of children and husband I guess – a
dimension of life I never experienced. I have also learned to be
honest in care giving and not pretend to be "caring" when I am
weary and in need of care myself. I always thought I had to be
thoughtful and available even if I felt emotionally bereft. Now I
know how unrealistic that is and dishonest too. You can't live
with someone all the time without friction.

*"I wake from sleep, and take my waking slow: I
learn by going where I have to go."*
                                            Theodore Roethke

*"Oh wad some power the giftie gie us
To see oursel's as ithers see us."*
Robert Burns

I thought I was pretty cool at the Friday night dances at the resort where my family vacationed, even though I often brought my depressed sister. She drank pop and danced once in a while, while I met lots of guys and danced all night. There was one guy I danced with several weeks in a row and I really liked him. One night, out of the clear blue sky, he said, "You act different when your sister is around." I was floored. "Like what?" "I don't know, you're more docile or subdued or something." He hesitated and I could tell he thought me more enjoyable when my sister was **not** there. This came as a complete shock to me. I certainly didn't feel any different whether Paula came with me or not, so how on earth could I appear to have changed? I felt chagrin and anxiety and it dawned on me that I could never be certain I appeared the way I thought I was. Later, I became aware that my sister's handicaps did bring out a protectiveness in me. So? So, the next summer I met a guy who never minded a bit if Paula came with us swimming or golfing or whatever. Now he's my husband.

We are subtly affected by each other far more than is apparent to ourselves. Our attitudes come through to others whether we intend it or not. On a subliminal level we convey messages and the truth will come out in the end. That is why we must tend our interior thoughts and cultivate those attitudes we really want. Sooner or later, it will show in our behavior.

*"If 'Thank You' were the only prayer ever said it
would be sufficient."*

                                            Meister Eckhart

We always called her the Cracker Jack Lady. We looked forward
to seeing her. My dad, a psychiatrist, worked at the state hospital,
and we were living in a white frame house on the grounds until
we could find a permanent home. We had just moved to a new
state; everything seemed strange to me. I was in first grade and
one day my brothers, sister and I were sledding on a little hill by
the house when she came over and gave me a toy bugle from a
box of Cracker Jacks. After that it became a regular ritual. When
she saw us playing, over she would come, fish around in her
baggy jacket pockets and produce a Cracker Jack favor, sometimes two or three. She is one of my earliest and fondest memories of my new home, even though Grandma was horrified that we
were allowed to "mingle with the patients." Her Cracker Jack
offerings said, "welcome." Maybe she could tell how important
she was from the way we fussed over whose turn it was to keep
the favor. Whenever I think of her, I hope she realized how happy
she made me feel.

**Small gestures and seemingly inconsequential events can bring
love and happiness into one's life. Those who have little can teach
us how little we really need to enjoy life. It is our own ever increasing wants that make us unhappy. Contentment consists not
in getting what we want but in giving thanks for what we have.**

"I understand a fury in your words, but not your words."
Shakespeare

What have I learned from dealing with my manic-depressive relative? Most important and also the hardest was learning to look beyond words to feelings. I am a literal, logical person and always got stuck in refuting the irrational words of my mate, all to no avail. Now, for example, I react only to the irritable mood that the words signal. This has helped me in relating to other people. Words can become exercises in conflict. Empathy for the emotion behind the words can bring down barriers and win understanding. It has become a new way for me to look at people. I am aware of my own feelings more now and allow myself to feel them and be in touch with them. Before, I squashed and denied them in my hurry to do and accomplish all the time and "be reasonable", and to take everything literally.

"You think too much! Clever men and grocers –
they weigh everything."

Zorba the Greek

When I find myself figuring, analyzing, weighing words full of fury, I think of Zorba. I try to cut through to the reality behind the words. I try to relate to what feelings this person is conveying.

"No man's knowledge can go beyond his experience."
John Locke

My husband counselled mentally ill persons and through him, I felt that I was knowledgeable about these illnesses. In fact I thought I knew quite a lot since I read professional journals with him and heard him discuss cases. One day a man came to repair the cement floor in our basement. He worked for a few hours in complete silence and I went to see how he was progressing. As I spoke with him, he noticed a picture of a bagpiper on the wall and started to tell me of his war experiences in World War II when he was stationed in Scotland for awhile. As he talked his voice became increasingly shrill and angry. The words boiled out of him. "The end of the world is coming. Doom to the fornicators and war mongers." A tirade on sin followed, with frequent pointing to his watch to emphasize "the time was near." My legs quivered and the more agitated he became the more like lead they felt. So **this** was how it is? I guessed he suffered from Post Traumatic Stress Disorder and was reliving war memories, but that didn't help me. I wondered if perhaps he planned to sink the trowel into my head! This was my first real live experience with mental illness.

My husband had arrived for lunch by now and came downstairs. He said quite simply, "Say, how about a cup of tea? Take a break. It's lunch time." The cement man clicked off abruptly, re-entered the world of the present and picked up his tool box. "No, no thanks. I'm done for today." He walked quietly up the stairs.

Knowledge without experience is incomplete. Imagine a doctor who only read books and never had any clinical training. What good is knowledge without the wisdom that comes from experience? Our perception of others is lacking until we allow ourselves to directly encounter those "others" who are different. Only then will our knowledge be fruitful.

"No behavior is despised by everybody."

Grandma has Alzheimer's disease and much of her behavior is
distressing and embarrassing. Not the least of these is her urinat-
ing in inappropriate places, necessitating the use of absorbent
undergarments. My five year old still occasionally wets his pants
and he does not despise Grandma's incontinence. On the contrary
he finds it a special bond, an understanding. He knows that
Grandma knows what it is like to pee your pants to the annoyance
of others. He sits by her and she pats his hand, the friendship a
humble boon to both.

"Company in distress makes the sorrow less."
Thomas Fuller

> *"Great wits are sure to madness near ally'd*
> *And thin partitions do their bounds*
> *divide."*
>   **John Dryden**

Dr. Kay Redfield Jamison studies the high proportion of mood disorders among poets, writers and artists. There seems to be a link between Bi-Polar (Manic-Depressive) Disorder and creativity in some families. Despite the inheritability of this disease, indeed, perhaps because of it, many members of such families are extremely successful. Relatives of Bi-Polar patients often show greater creativity than average people. It is as though something is inherited in a milder form that fosters creativity, while a more severe form disables their sick relative. These genes may be transmitting not only disease but benefits.

We are all linked one to another. The traits that my sick relative has may be linked to genes that benefit me in some way. But for a speck of molecule in a different amount in him, there, but for the grace of God, go I.

"A handful of patience is worth a bushel of brains."
Dutch proverb

My co-workers and family have called me "General" (or Hitler!) because I tend to dominate, judge, expect perfection. My son's eight year struggle with chronic schizophrenia has forced a change in me. I no longer snarl at a less than bright secretary or a sales clerk, nor do I grimace with annoyance at street people (whom I used to call "bums"). I nod and smile at some mumbling old decrepit at the bus stop, for one of them could be my son. I remember Jim roaming from halfway houses and trying to get a part time job at our local hardware store. I remember the times he wore filthy shabby jeans and pasted tattoos all over his arms. I see him now carefully doling out three medications every morning and struggling to learn social skills that he once took for granted.

"Patience is the best remedy for a sick person."
John Florio

For people who are quick, intelligent, and capable, patience with those who have a disability is a slow and hard lesson. Yet it is the greatest gift we can extend to the handicapped, and perhaps the greatest gift they give to us. They teach us to temper our demands for instant relief, to bear with tedium and slow results. They add the dimension of patience to our hurried personalities and we are healthier for that.

*"She wears her clothes as if they were thrown on
with a pitchfork."*
                                        Jonathan Swift

I dreaded my friends seeing mother. Her outfits were flamboyant
and disheveled, drawing attention like a flag to her provocative
speech. I never knew when she would swear or insult or ask
impossible questions. Someone would say, "I saw your mom in
Wal-Mart's" and I'd immediately freeze in terror. What's next?
Even though my mind knew she was hypomanic, I felt mortified
because my esteem rested on the shaky foundations of peer
acceptance. **Their** parents seemed so normal. At least they
dressed in a conventional way, and how else can you tell people
are "normal" when you see them? At least, I thought, if Mom's
attire were subdued, people may not notice her behavior.

**In our culture, self esteem is bound to appearances. Regardless
of the proverbial admonishment, we do "judge a book by its
cover". A Chinese proverb says, "A really rich man is careless
of his dress." I ponder this. It could mean a very wealthy person
can afford to flaunt what he considers petty proprieties. Or it
could mean a person who is rich in spirit and inner values, does
not waste much time fussing over the outer shell. I have learned
to not overvalue appearances.**

"There is a pleasure sure in being mad which none but madmen know."

John Dryden

Poets who suffer from mental illness often describe the peculiar lure of the illness. For example, Edgar Allan Poe writes, "I fell in love with melancholy." William Blake says, "Under every grief and pine, runs a joy with silken twine."

An old lady rocking in her chair will laugh at her voices because they amuse her. Another will miss his manic episodes following treatment. Who wouldn't want to feel like Superman or Wonder Woman?

My cousin, who was schizo-affective, was riding in the car with a group of us on a gloomy day in March. Suddenly, she laughed and said with great hilarity, "The sun's out! Look at the sun." Busily talking we ignored her because she was staring at the floor. But, sure enough, a ray of light was reflecting off a brass shoe buckle as the sun broke through the clouds.

Who knows what insights or connections a mentally ill person may perceive that elude us "normals"?

"A wise man is often he who does not in the least think he is."

Boileau

The reality of the mentally ill may be different from ours, but there is still validity in their experience. They may access truths about life and philosophy and the earth that we do not. Their struggles are not without redemption.

*"To thine own self be true...and thou canst be
false to no man."*
Shakespeare

Larry's hair and beard wreathed his sharp features like cobwebs.
He often sunned himself at the picnic table in front of Building 7
and it was there I first greeted him. My dad was a social worker
and I picked him up after work. He stopped to ask Larry how
things were going. Soon we were talking about me and school – I
was in tenth grade. "Are you going to be a social worker like
your dad here?" asked Larry. "Or maybe a psychiatrist like Dr.
Parkins?" He pointed a bony, tobacco stained finger at the doctor
crossing the lawn. "I keep telling him that's **exactly** what he
should do – he's a bright boy," Dad jumped in. "Go into medicine."

I scowled. We have been through all this before. I wanted to be a
journalist - maybe write books some day. I can't stand sick
people and most of all detest psychology and the sciences!

"No, I don't think so," I said to Larry. "I want to be a writer."

He straightened up and looked at me fiercely with his long finger
pointed right at my nose. "You do what you want to do," he
exclaimed, "and don't let this guy (an elbow at Dad) or anyone
else decide what you are going to do! Ya understand that, Son?"
His head shook vigorously. "Yessir, you do what you want!"

After that, every time I saw Larry, he waved and called, "Remember what I told you; do what you want to!" Because it was so
spontaneous, hearty and unreserved, his advice and encouragement touched me. The words were a good omen, opportune and
artless. I valued them all the more because of that.

*"Speak your truth quietly and clearly. Listen to
others, even the dull or ignorant, for they too have
a story."*
Max Ehrmann, <u>Desiderata</u>

WAYS TO HELP

"I WOULD BRING BALM AND POUR IT INTO YOUR WOUND – CURE YOUR DISTEMPERED MIND AND HEAL YOUR FORTUNE."

JOHN DRYDEN

"NOT ALL THERE"

She's not "all there" say the neighbors
As they go about their labors:
Selling, managing, making stuff;
Scrambling for bucks - there's not enough!

> *I'm not "all there" for you to see,*
> *The vessel's broke that carries me.*
> *It filters my existence through*
> *cracks all strained and twisted.*

She sees, but does not perceive;
She thinks, but the thoughts are
Disconnected and distorted
Rationality aborted.

> *Yet truly I know I am here,*
> *A kindly word fills me with cheer.*
> *I love the flowers blue and red,*
> *Admire the white clouds overhead.*

She's not "all there", and yet SOMEWHERE,
For of this fact we are aware,
When the medicine works, why then,
She reappears, whole again!

> *"Not all there" - I disagree.*
> *I'm here in my entirety:*
> *My heart thrills to a marching band,*
> *Laughter and tears I understand.*

> *"Not all there" - don't be misled.*
> *You cannot know me with your head.*
> *But we are not that far apart.*
> *You can know me with your heart.*

Mary Brust Heaney

"The terrible burden having nothing to do."
N. Boileau-Despreaux

A woman criticized our neighbor for "using" her mentally ill son as free maintenance man and gardener. His mother seemed to always have him repairing things, mowing or raking, or painting. My friend thought he should be working and having social life away from home. I do not know whether he was capable of being away from home, but I do know he took great pride in his jobs, and enjoyed the compliments they earned. There are communities in Europe where the mentally handicapped work and take care of themselves, even marginally, and live a satisfying life, regardless of how ill they may be. The important thing is that they **all** contribute something.

In our society, finding employment is probably the most effective yet the most elusive therapy for the mentally ill. I will make sure I find something for my loved one to do. To be excluded from the world of work and duty is no favor – it is a Terrible Burden!

"The diseases of the mind are more destructive
than those of the body."
                                        Marcus Cicero

This observation was made over two thousand years ago. The
destructiveness I believe Cicero meant is the blocking of relationships, and the person's connectedness to the world. How can I
know and relate meaningfully to you if you are a stranger, locked
in a world apart? That "insane root that takes the reason prisoner"
seems to thwart what is most essential to being human: rationality,
the ability to have meaningful dialogue.

That makes it all the more crucial for me to maintain the link,
despite absent or inappropriate feedback. Who knows how often
a smile, a stroll together, a pleasant phrase lingers in memory like
a seed of hope? Once these actions touch the heart, they are never
lost. There are ways to relate that do not depend upon intellect
and reason.

"I have three things to teach: compassion,
patience, simplicity."
                                        Lao-Tze

**I will never underestimate the power of a touch, a word, a lis-
tening ear. I will remember that it is far more important to have
a heart that is kind than an abundance of knowledge in the mind,
for it is not the intellect that makes one human, but the ability
to give and receive love.**

Mary Heaney

"Better be friends at a distance than enemies at home."
Scottish proverb

Grandpa's Alzheimer's disease progressively became harder and harder to cope with at home. His loss of functioning was very painful for us all. Our kids resented his hostile outbursts and irascible tongue. He wandered unpredictably, sometimes getting lost for hours. We agonized over the decision to place him in a nursing home. Other people seemed to manage long term care in their homes. My siblings, who lived a great distance away, wondered if the move was impulsive and premature.

At first, he seemed unhappy and disoriented, provoking guilt. But now, I know our decision was the right one. Our kids visit twice a week to the enjoyment of everyone. They play games and read to him. We take Grandpa on outings and he comes home for special occasions and holidays. A relationship that was deteriorating into mutual resentment has survived despite the fact that his condition on the whole is deteriorating.

I've heard it said that Alzheimer's disease is that condition in which the mind and the body decide to die at different times. Yet it is not so simple. The brain is the body as much as the liver or stomach. The impact of brain diseases on relationships may be more immediate and striking, but cancer and heart disease also affect relationships, and every organ affects every other.

"Better are works when the heart is joyous."
                                    <u>The Wisdom of Amenemope</u>

Mom knocked herself out doing things for Lelia. She enrolled her
in art classes, dressed her tastefully, kept her busy in the garden.
Mom was president of the community womens' club and active in
our church. She dreaded her friends and neighbors discovering
Lelia had schizophrenia. She hushed her abruptly when folks
visited. In spite of Mom's obvious concern and helpfulness, she
often became irritable, impatient, and critical with Lelia. Her
focus centered on that nebulous time in the future when her
daughter would finally be "well".

Once a month, Aunt Liz visited. "Lelia, dear, how are you? How
nice to see you." Her eyes gleamed as they sat and talked and Liz
laughed at Lelia's stupid jokes, which she repeated every time,
and when she took leave, she left a bright red lipstick mark on
Lelia's cheek. They had not a single activity or interest in common. Their shared humanity was enough to raise Lelia's shoul-
ders, put a smile on her lips and set her glowing with peace.

**Sometimes our anxiety and pride prevent us from the one thing
we as family members can offer: humble acceptance of their
brokenness. It's not that we don't help in many ways, or that
these interventions are not necessary and helpful. But simply
sharing and accepting is the element that enhances all others.**

"Whence comes it that a cripple does not irritate us, and a crippled mind does irritate us?"

It is because the cripple knows and recognizes that he is crooked and we are straight. But the crippled mind does not recognize his illness and says it is we who limp. How desperately people resist accepting the fact of a mental illness. Besides the pain of knowing how limited and circumscribed their lives may become, there is the social stigma to deal with. Sometimes by refusing treatment or neglecting to take their medication, they hope to prove they are not "mental". Accepting that one has a mental illness is easier said than done.

Sometimes delusions make it difficult to trust doctors and other care givers. Normal reasoning may be beyond one's scope. It may take weeks or months to help a sick person accept his need for long term help.

If I understand that the crippled mind is truly as needy as the cripple, I will pity rather than be angry with him. I can help by keeping clear in my own mind the positive benefits that will result from treatment and medication. With patience and fortitude, my confidence will eventually rub off, and help him to stick with treatment.

"Be of good courage and he shall strengthen your heart."
Psalm 31

"Would it not grieve a woman to be mastered by a piece of valiant dust?"

Shakespeare,
Much Ado About Nothing

Dust certainly will not master my wife. She is a big-time washer and cleaner, like four hours a day. Before she was on medication, she could not sit for fifteen minutes without finding something to wash. She would walk around the room looking for lint to pick off the rug. I can tell you most certainly that cleanliness is NOT next to Godliness, even though my neighbors admire our spotless home! To keep Susie from spending all night cleaning up the kitchen, I SET A TIMER and she finally has been able to stop when the timer goes off. Without her medication I don't think setting limits would have succeeded. Sometimes I find **myself** obsessing and ruminating about **her** illness! What helps me to stop obsessive thinking is to get moving – I take a walk or distract myself with a crossword puzzle.

Our culture seems kinder to obsessive-compulsives more than other mental illnesses. Cleanliness is a virtue and excessive thinking is being conscientious. But as anyone who lives with this disorder knows, it destroys the spontaneity of life. Helping to set time limits on compulsive rituals is one way to get relief. "Thought stopping" is another aid. This is accomplished by immediate and deliberate deflection away from the obsessions by turning to some physical activity or mental challenge. It's important to spot obsessive thinking because once you're on the train, it doesn't stop!

"I am but mad north - north - west. When the wind is southerly I know a hawk from a hand-saw."
Shakespeare

Unlike the above quote, people with mental illness have difficulty seeing how events and circumstances affect their symptoms. They do not connect an exacerbation of symptoms with a particular stress in their environment, whether it be a change in the weather, a holiday, a certain person. If we notice that a change in their behavior is connected to something in the environment, it helps to make a quiet observation, although they may not agree with you. Helping them recognize and deal with stress is a major contribution on our part.

I will strive to learn how to recognize early signs of stress and deterioration and meet them without alarm. Likewise, I will learn to recognize even tiny signs of improvement, and offer encouragement and recognition.

"To yield reverence to another, to hold ourselves at his disposal, is not slavery: it is the noblest state in which a person can live in this world."
John Ruskin

In this age of "self-fulfillment", there often is not much empathy for those who care for sick family members. Solicitude and responsibility are viewed as impediments to self-actualization. But what is more precious than meeting someone's needs of the moment with an attitude of love? For it's all in the attitude. As long as we feel put upon and cheated, we will be disappointed and unhappy. But suppose we rejoice in the service, seeing it not as a frustration but an opportunity to learn and grow. An attitude of grudging compliance invites disappointment. An attitude recognizing the intrinsic value of our service invites moments of joy. It makes us grateful for our own gifts, and the opportunity to use them.

"Life is not worthwhile unless it is lived for others."
Mother Theresa

"The gloom of the world is but a shadow;
Behind it, yet within reach, Is joy. Take joy."
                              Fra Giovanni, 16th century

Depression afflicts one of my best friends. I have listened to his negative ruminations for hours in an effort to be kind and supportive. There were times when all I wanted was to go to sleep but I hung in there past midnight listening, listening, trying to turn around his gloomy thinking. In so doing, I ended up dejected myself; he really got me down. Then I felt angry and hostile.

One day I interrupted, "I can't be around you now. I can't handle all this 'crepe-hanging' and misery you wallow in. I know you have a hard time changing your thoughts, but I need time out!" Like a great gray cloud floating away, my mind cleared of irritation and I put a Rossini overture on the stereo and turned up the volume. Since that day, I have realized that authentic love and charity depend on honesty, not on faking solicitude when it overburdens me. Setting tactful limits has made me a more reliable friend.

Taking joy for ourselves benefits others. Joy radiates and peace is contagious. Read humorous stories, buy a bouquet, sink into a hot bath, enjoy a concert, wander through a park. Take joy for yourself before you consider taking care of others. It's the best way to help them too.

*"An ugly voice can be heard farther than a
beautiful one."*
Slavic proverb

People with mental illness are exquisitely sensitive to the emotional climate. They read nuances in voice, body language, and may react disproportionately. For example, a sharp or loud request may be viewed as a demand and provoke negative reaction. It is best to ask, not tell, when something needs to be done. Getting eye contact and showing respect enhances cooperation.

A corollary to this is the fact that persons with mental illness seem to remember negative events and exchanges much more than positive ones. Even in milder forms of depression this is common, as sad thoughts sprout like uncontrollable weeds.

Emphasize appreciation, smile requests, explain the positive benefits of acting in a desirable way. Avoid carping criticism, giving orders, saying what is wrong all the time. Wouldn't this benefit all of us?

"I praise loudly; I blame softly."
Catherine II of Russia

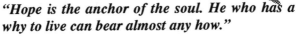

*"Hope is the anchor of the soul. He who has a
why to live can bear almost any how."*
Fred. Nietzsche

Dante said of Hell, "Abandon hope, all ye who enter here." Hope
is what often prevents someone from slipping into the abyss of
despair, suicide. The hope held out by a family member or friend,
an understanding aide, a fellow patient, a nurse or doctor or social
worker becomes a link in the chain that anchors a soul to life.
When a tortured person sees no reason to live in pain it's up to
anyone to help him through this moment, and the next and the
next. The assurance that someone wants him to live may anchor a
person. Someone telling him to bear the moment because the act
that looks like a solution can never be undone and tomorrow will
come may halt despair.

*"Beware of desperate steps. The darkest day
(Live til tomorrow) will have passed away."*
Wm. Cowper

*"Mind and body affect each other. There is con-
tinuing reaction between them so that if pain is
lessened on either side you diminish the pain of
both; if improvement on one side, both improve."*
Leigh Hunt, 1820

There seems to be a persistent notion that someone who is mentally ill is impervious to physical surroundings. My aunt never
thought to replace her depressed son's bed even though the
springs sagged and the mattress slumped pitifully. She assumed
that since he mentally is in his own world, his body must be also.

While it is true that a person with mental illness may neglect
grooming and be sloppy about household objects, anything we do
to improve this situation is not without positive consequences.
Developing a routine for dressing, providing attractive, comfort-
able clothes, insisting they keep themselves and their living space
clean helps not only one's body but the mind. Pleasant, attractive
surroundings and nutritious food soothe the mental and physical
alike. Exercise, gardens, family gatherings, social events greatly
improve the quality of life for mentally ill persons, even though
they may appear indifferent.

*"Who will tell whether the joy of breathing or
walking on a bright morning or smelling the fragrance of flowers in the air is not worth all the
suffering and effort which life implies?"*
Erich Fromm

*"Consider well what your strength is equal to, and
what exceeds your ability."*

Horace

To give my mother some respite, I offered to bring my sister
home with me for two weeks. My husband is easy going and my
kids were busy with school and friends. Even so, I found myself
exhausted after three days. Her incessant talking about the
mysteries of the universe and secret plans the government had to
imbed micro chips into everyone got on my nerves. I could not
handle her hostile outbursts, and even when she stayed in her
room for hours, my nerves were on edge. Our other sister doesn't
seem all that bothered by this. She has a knack for shutting
herself off and ignoring almost anything. She is the one who has
embraced zen meditation in our family.

So back to Mother's. We finally made an arrangement that I
would drive Trudy whenever she needed to go somewhere, and
take her shopping and to the movies. Lois can bring her home for
hours or days at a time and do the listening. Our brother, a
professional by the way, has no contact whatsoever, but he does
send money, so I guess we all do what we can.

Where there is sincere desire to help, ways will be found.

*"I will work in my own way, according to the light
that is in me."*

Lydia Maria Child

"How little do they see what really is,
Who frame their hasty judgment on what seems?"
R. Southey

We often became annoyed with our sister in law, Debbie. She seemed unfriendly and often was curt when she spoke. Or she would just sit and stare into space, as if she didn't want to be around us. Other times all she did was complain. We felt offended. Who did she think she was? What kind of a family member was this? Then, remarkably, her mood improved and she confided to me she was seeing a therapist and was taking antidepressants and how much better she was feeling. Suddenly she wasn't such a bitch after all – and it was all in the way I looked at her.

If someone is blind, we don't expect him to read. Yet we automatically expect those related to us to be kind, loving, interested, sociable. We do not know what problems they may be having.

I will try to reserve judgment on difficult people. Why do I think they are deliberately annoying me when they may be wrestling with their own demons?

"Ask yourself daily, to how many ill-minded persons
you have shown a kind disposition."
Marcus Aurelius

OBSERVATIONS AND MISCONCEPTIONS

"WHEN IN DISGRACE WITH FORTUNE
        AND MEN'S EYES
I ALL ALONE BEWEEP MY OUTCAST STATE
AND LOOK UPON MYSELF AND CURSE MY FATE..."
                                Shakespeare

"Psychiatrists are continually discovering that what seems abnormal behavior is really a normal reaction to abnormal surroundings."
Dr. Earl D. Bond

To see your buddy's limbs ripped off from an exploding bomb, to hear the screams of agony as a fellow prisoner is tortured, to feel your favorite uncle's body pressing down on your five-year-old pelvis...is there a "normal" way to react to these circumstances? Nightmares, disassociation, depression, rage – are not these sometimes "normal" reactions to abhorrent and aberrant situations? Wouldn't it be abnormal NOT to react in extreme ways to inhuman events? To not become "crazy" under certain circumstances may be another form of madness!

Never assume immunity from mental disturbances. May I recognize my own propensity for illness, given the trigger of terrible circumstances.

"It is now clearly comprehended that any illness, even though it may appear to be restricted to the physical, nevertheless, always contains a mental component which must be appreciated and treated."

Dr. Edward Strecker

The mentally ill are not a " race apart". They have a more severe or chronic degree of symptoms and abnormalities that affect their behavior and perception. But stroke patients get depressed, multiple sclerosis and arteriosclerotic patients can get manic symptoms, even flu victims suffer temporary depression. Psychotic reactions may occur with anesthesia or cold medicines. Catatonia has occurred in lupus and malignancies. We cannot separate our biology and our minds. Even Scrooge acknowledged this when he suspected his ghosts may be "a scrap of undigested potato."

"Our mental conditions are simply symbols in consciousness of the changes taking place automatically in the organism."

T. H. Huxley, 1874

*"Major mental illness is a 'no-fault disease' that
requires a supportive environment and proper
medication."*

**Laurie M. Flynn, Executive Director
National Alliance for the Mentally Ill**

Recent studies of schizophrenics who receive comprehensive
psychosocial rehabilitation along with their medication are very
encouraging. There is a much higher recovery rate than generally
acknowledged. Even very sick, chronically ill people show
significant improvement. As many as 50 percent of them have a
good chance of substantial progress in community living skills. A
New England study of de-institutionalized patients covering three
decades concluded that a large percentage of them can, and do,
show remarkable improvement given the proper environment and
support system along with their medications. Community support
programs provide the least expensive and best treatment.

**We've come a long way from the old days when treatment meant
not so much to cure as to "secure". There is a movement towards day hospitals, half-way houses and other interim supervised living places. However, they are few compared to the need.
The homeless mentally ill are on the streets by default. Studies
have indicated that when they receive ongoing outpatient treatment, the homeless mentally ill do not return to the streets but
stay in supervised living when available.**

*"We both read the Bible day and night. But where
thou reads black, I read white."*
                                    Wm. Blake

It wasn't so long ago that mental illness was considered a moral disease. You were possessed by the devil. Or you had no backbone or character. Or you were paying for sins of your parents. The "immoral acts" of the mentally ill horrified people. After all, they scream obscenities, act abusive, throw lamps and stab themselves. What righteous Christian acts like that! This is the Bible read "black".

There are those who heed the call to compassion, the call to befriend those who are outcasts, the call to forgive and reconcile, and ease pain rather than condemn and criticize. This is the Bible read "white".

*"One word frees us of all the weight and pain of
life: That word is love."*
                                    Sophocles, 406 B.C.

"Canst thou not minister to a mind diseased?
Pluck from the memory a rooted sorrow? Raze
out the troubles of the brain?"
Shakespeare

I have a picture of Bedlam Hospital in the 1700's. It shows a withered man chained to a bed, his knees drawn up, nightshirt pulled all around, staring vacantly. Every time I look at it, I am grateful for the progress that has been made in the treatment of the mentally ill. More effective medicines with fewer side effects are appearing with remarkable regularity. Knowledge of brain chemistry and chemical imbalance is expanding so that never before has hope loomed so brightly for the mentally ill to live in their communities.

I am grateful for all those who minister to diseased minds and for all those who make available the money and the means with which to do it. If financial support for mental illness would only parallel the strides being made in treatment. What an irony it is that the more progress is made in treatment, the less chance to implement it due to stingy and inequable funding!

"Egotism is the anesthetic that dulls the pain of stupidity."
Frank Leahy

They do not have a "mental illness". These are the ones who are just ignorant enough to feel superior, just charitable enough to be ingratiating, just indifferent enough to be inhumane. These are the people who have no "mental symptoms", never knew a mental patient, think the right thoughts and lead the good life, even do good works. They present a face of confidence, success, enlightenment, fun, and self-righteousness. Blinded by their own egos, they are blind to others. "Who is blinder than he who will not see?" As one friend put it, "They live in their own private hell."

The conclusion seems obvious: The mental cases most difficult to treat are the people who are crazy about themselves!

"Most ignorance is vincible ignorance. We don't know because we don't want to know."
Aldous Huxley

"I teach that all men are crazy."
Horace, 25 B.C.

Horace probably recognized that we all have our quirks and at some time or another think irrationally, have poor judgment, or behave idiotically.

If he lived today, he would not be surprised that six million Americans suffer from serious mental illness. The mentally ill occupy more hospital beds than patients with diabetes, heart disease, cancer, and arthritis combined! Treatment reduces symptoms, but no "cures" are known. Mental illness puts enormous strains on families. Meanwhile, funding is woefully inadequate, prejudice and stigma widespread, indicating another sort of "craziness" in our society!

Don't you think it is "crazy" that we as a people try to ignore a medical and social problem of this magnitude?

"Out of sight, out of mind" was translated into Russian (by computer). When it was then translated back to English it read "Invisible Maniac". It strikes me that a lot of people translate mental illness this way. "Out of sight, out of mind" is interpreted "Out of mind, out of sight". Hide the mentally ill, then we can ignore them.

"Nothing in life is to be feared. It is only to be understood."
Marie Curie

Fear breeds cruelty. We hate what we fear. On a TV talk show, a woman described her ordeal with her husband's suicidal depression. She told how he had disappeared for several days, not knowing where he had gone, being mad with worry. His depression had been unknown until he returned and was hospitalized. He admitted he had suicidal thoughts many times and felt he had to "keep up a front" and not be "weak." For many months he tried to function without confiding to anyone the extent of his anguish. So he staged a fake burglary of his car and disappeared, the tacit conclusion being he had met with some tragedy.

It amazed me how many people in the audience asked why didn't she divorce him. Even after his treatment and favorable prognosis was discussed, many felt she should leave him for all the misery he had caused the family. Would they have advised this if he had a stroke? If he had incurable cancer? If he had chronic diabetes, Alzheimers?

Somehow the idea persists that depression is deliberate; the person is culpable. We say, "Get a grip on yourself." Which is of course exactly what this man attempted, with disastrous consequences. Had he realized the remarkable availability of treatment, he may have sought help sooner. If those around him recognized an illness and knew there was treatment available they may have acted differently, too!

Madame Curie and other scientists spent their lives researching the realm of human ignorance. Ralph B. Perry said that, "Ignorance deprives men of freedom, because they do not know what alternatives there are. How can you choose to do what you have never heard of?"

"Diseased nature oftentimes breaks forth
In strange eruptions."
Shakespeare

Mental illness may mystify, but stranger still are life's interventions, like rocking chairs. Harry suffered manic-depressive illness. Impulsive behavior and substance abuse contribute to a high rate of suicide, often unintentional, in those with this illness. Harry was one of the lucky ones. At the height of a manic episode, he drank heavily and his sexual episodes were reckless. He was invincible; he could leap tall buildings with a single bound. One night he stormed out of a confrontation between his wife and latest paramour, secluded himself in the den and started on a bottle of vodka. Soon his mother-in-law's shrill voice joined in the acrimonious accusations in the kitchen.

"The hell with it all," his alcohol-soaked brain decided. Pulling a revolver from the desk drawer, he held it to his head and fired one shot, a second, a third. Missed all three times. Harry was in his rocking chair and with each rock the bullet just grazed his hair. His death foiled by a rocking chair, Harry was hospitalized, properly diagnosed, and eventually stabilized on lithium and anti-convulsants. He did not become an "accidental death" or a suicide statistic.

The mortality rate for untreated manic-depressive illness is higher than for many forms of heart disease and cancer. This is often a result of substance abuse, risk-taking behavior, impulsivity, and poor judgement.

*"It is not by confining one's neighbor that one is
convinced of one's own sanity."*
Dostoievsky

One of our more irrational ways of thinking is "either - or",
"black or white". If **you're** insane, **I** must be sane. If **you** are
bad, **I** am good. If **you** are wrong, **I** am right. If I can show **your**
shortcomings, **mine** are non-existent. Alas, none of these conclu-
sions is valid. If the prisons are full, we think we are safe from
crimes; if the deranged are sequestered out of sight, the rest of us
are sane and normal and healthy. Maybe so, maybe not.

Making judgments on others does not in itself guarantee anything
about ourselves. Such thinking is that of a young adolescent,
whose identity rests on opposition. "I'm not what my parents
are." But that still doesn't give the security of knowing, "Who am
I?" Constructing one's ego from comparison to others is like
building on quicksand.

*"What we really are matters more than what other
people think of us."*
Jawaharlal Nehru

"Chance has something to say in everything, even writing a good letter."

Baltasar Gracian

Two of my children have suffered severe depression. When they get depressed, I hear about all the bad things that happened in their childhood, all the arguments, the misunderstandings, all the mistakes and cruelties. Their tears and accusations make me feel awful, even though I know all parents do stupid things and have limitations.

Early family environmental factors as the cause of one's mental health has been overdone, in my opinion. I for one am glad to hear of research pointing to hereditary factors involving faulty brain transmitter substances. At least I feel less burdened. After all, genes are a roll of the dice – what can I do about that?

Two recent independent studies involving over 20,000 twins, siblings, and other relatives came to the conclusion that depression appears to be highly heritable and that childhood environmental factors are not as paramount as supposed in the development of adult depression. This is a turn-about from traditional thinking! (*APA Journal*, Dec. 1994)

"Prithee," the fool addresses King Lear, "tell me
whether a madman be a gentleman or a yeoman."
"A King," Lear replies, "a King."
Shakespeare, <u>King Lear</u>

Charles VI of France apparently suffered from schizophrenia while Philip V of Spain was thought to have manic-depression and Winston Churchill endured bouts of severe depression. King or slave, wealthy or poor, educated or not, mental illness plays no favorites.

"I envied a wealthy acquaintance," a man confided. "He had a successful business, a mansion to live in, handsome children, travelled wherever he pleased. His gifted life irked my jealous mind. It didn't seem fair for me to struggle so much while someone else with similar education and background had it so good. Then quite by accident one day I learned that he was receiving ECT treatments for the fifth time. He had regular bouts of severe depression which required several series of shock treatments, greatly distressing and disrupting himself and his family.

"I was dumbfounded. Never again could I smugly envy the good fortune of another with impunity."

"Nature in disease is consistent and uniform, so that you
observe in the sickness of Socrates the selfsame symptoms
as in the sickness of a simple man."
Thomas Sydenham

"Anyone who has a brain is liable to insanity precisely as everyone with lungs is liable to pneumonia."

Dr. Thomas Kirkbride

The Russian physician and writer Anton Chekov made the astute observation that denial of biological origins for mental symptoms is extremely common among patients and families. He accurately described the symptoms of brain pathology, in particular Bi-polar (manic-depressive) illness. He was struck by how often everyone ascribes the symptoms to everything **but biology**, whether it be diet, weather, faulty upbringing, or supernatural causes. This was particularly true in his day, but even today many are reluctant to recognize the genetic and biological basis of mental illness. It seems easier to blame someone or something in the environment, moral degeneration, or look to the past for explanations. Of course negative influences may contribute to an illness, but today we know that the biological vulnerability comes first.

As far back as the fifth century B. C., bodily "humours" were thought to effect mental illnesses, particularly "black bile". The thread of physical cause has run through the history of treatment. Today Chekov's timeless truths are resurging with the explosion in brain research and increasing knowledge of brain chemistry. Treatments for mental illnesses have never been more promising.

Mary Heaney

"What are fears but voices airy?
Whispering harm where harm is not."
Wordsworth

Fears of violence block the acceptance into the community of those with serious mental illness. The prevalent attitude is that they are dangerous. This is true of only a tiny percentage of the mentally ill. There is far more potential and actual violence from alcohol and substance abusers who remain an unchallenged and normal part of every community. We do not demand that they all be sequestered for our safety. Yet this group has by far the greatest actual record of violent episodes.

Only about 11% of schizophrenics and manic-depressives had a violent episode during a one-year long study. The figure rose to 25% with alcohol or substance abuse, and 38% with both alcohol and drug use.

With more effective medications to control symptoms, the safety margin for the mentally ill narrows yearly, provided they do not become substance abusers. Thus to fear them solely on their illness is exaggeration.

"I am a man more sinned against than sinning."
Shakespeare

"No man is an island entire of itself."
John Donne

Our attitudes and beliefs about a person have the power to elicit corresponding behavior. Beliefs shape actions. In the case of mentally disturbed people this is excruciatingly true. They are exquisitely sensitive to attitudes of others and respond accordingly. Thus if people expect them to be deviant and incompetent, this becomes a self-fulfilling prophecy. Mentally disabled persons believe that people devalue them. Stigma itself has a devastating effect.

It is crucial that we who are close to a mentally disadvantaged person view him as someone with strengths and weaknesses who can learn and improve. If we succumb to attitudes of disgrace and despair, we encourage him to perform more poorly than necessary. We can empower with an attitude of hope and acceptance. If we don't, who will? We are the ones who supply the only ongoing long term support and encouragement.

There is no better exercise for the heart than reaching down and lifting someone up.

*"Health of the mind is of far more importance
than health of the body."*
                                        Colton

We don't hear of telethons for schizophrenia or rock concerts for
depression. Funding for chronic mental illnesses remains woefully inadequate both for research and treatment. Insurance
companies remain reluctant to cover mental illnesses despite
growing evidence that it is cost effective. Can you imagine the
outcry if this were true of by-pass operations or cancer treatments
or arthritis?

Perhaps we should re-label these illnesses. Would "hyposero-
tonergic syndrome" for depression or "dopamine imbalance
disease" for schizophrenia, or "circadian rhythm dysfunction" for
mania make these diseases more amenable to funding? Should
not chronic chemical imbalance in the brain, like the chronic
chemical imbalance of diabetes, or the erratic growth of cancer
cells, be worthy of insurance coverage as well as research and
public support?

**How many times have we heard someone say, "I don't care about
growing old – just so I have my mind." Those whose brains are
disordered serve to remind us how fortunate we are. But there
is no guarantee that we will always be so lucky. Who knows
when you or I may have to say, like Jonathan Swift, *"I shall be
like a tree – I shall die starting at the top."***

"I never seed anybody but lied one time or another."
Mark Twain, <u>Huckleberry Finn</u>

Secrecy, lying, and caution are survival strategies for mental patients. Work is the most beneficial of therapies, but do you have any idea how difficult it is to find employment if your history is known? Or how formidable an undertaking it is to rent a place to live if the landlord finds out you are, or have been, a mental patient?

In the face of a hostile environment the only recourse for both patient and family is secrecy about the disability. This stigma compounds the problems and the loneliness. Indeed, it is worse than the illness.

So, as Zorba the Greek said, "I undo my belt and I fight!" If lies are part of the fight, so be it.

"Any fool can tell the truth, but it requires some sense to know how to lie well."
Samuel Butler

> *"At every word a reputation dies."*
> **Alexander Pope**

The words "mental illness" evoke a common prejudice. People who have sought treatment for mental illness are suspect, tainted, unreliable. Thus their reputation is destroyed despite the fact that millions of people with a mental illness function as responsible members of society.

Consider Paul's experience. He came under attack from his ex-wife in a custody battle over their son. Because he had been under treatment for severe depression and spent a short time in the hospital, her lawyers tried to discredit him, and give her full custody, despite the fact that Paul was now working and functioning well.

For every Paul, there are any number of alcoholics who are **not** seeking treatment, and people with severe mental problems who have never been to a doctor or therapist for their illness. Yet we all too often stigmatize those who **do** get help. Who is a better spouse, worker, parent – the one who receives help or the one who denies his problem or is too fearful of stigma to get the help he needs? Yet we continue to ignore what does not reinforce our prejudices. We see only what suits us.

> *"If you communicate your secret to another, you have made yourself his slave."*
> **Baltasar Gracian**

It's bad enough to be enslaved by the stigma of society, but how bitter when someone close uses one's illness to reject, to hold hostage, to threaten?

"IF I CAN STOP ONE HEART FROM
BREAKING
    I SHALL NOT LIVE IN VAIN
IF I CAN EASE ONE LIFE THE ACHING
       OR COOL ONE PAIN
       OR HELP ONE FAINTING ROBIN
UNTO HIS NEST AGAIN
    I SHALL NOT LIVE IN VAIN."

                          Emily Dickinson

EPILOGUE

Although we start out as strangers, I hope it will not always be so. To those completely unfamiliar with the world of mental illness, may the glimpses in these pages serve as an introduction. For you who already know someone who is mentally ill, I hope the result is increased understanding and comfort.

Our relationship with someone who has a mental illness reflects in a sharper image the paradox of *all* relationships. We are solitary, yet we need others. The fact that each of us is ultimately alone fills us with dread. At the same time, we fear the differences we see in others.

We remain strangers until we reach out with the hope of seeing and sharing our similarities. Thus, the stranger resides in each of us.

> *"It's not right to die before we've had a chance to share ourselves with each other."*
> **Thomas Jefferson, letter to John Adams**

RESOURCES

National Alliance for the Mentally Ill
2101 Wilson Boulevard
  Suite 302
Arlington, Virginia 22201
1-800-950-NAMI (1-800-950-6264)

National Mental Health Association
1021 Prince Street
Alexandria, Virginia 22314-2971
1-800-969-NMHA (1-800-969-6642)

National Depressive and Manic Depressive Association
730 North Franklin Street
  Suite 501
Chicago, Illinois 60610
1-800-82N DMNA (1-800-826-3632)

Anxiety Disorders Association of America (ADAA)
6000 Executive Boulevard
  Suite 513
Rockville, Maryland 20852-3801
1-301-231-9350

Obsessive-Compulsive Disorder Foundation
1-203-878-5669

BiPolar Network News
6001 Montrose Road
  Suite 809
Rockville, Maryland 20852

National Foundation for Depressive Illness, Inc.
P.O. Box 2257
New York, New York 10116
1-800-248-4344

National Alzheimer's Association
919 North Michigan Avenue
  Suite 1000
Chicago, Illinois 60611-1676
1-800-272-3900

INDEX

SUGGESTED READING

Books that deal with families of mentally ill:

Dickens, Rex & Marsh, Diana (1994). Anguished Voices: Personal Accounts of Siblings and Children. Center for Psychiatric Rehabilitation, 730 Commonwealth Ave. Boston, MA. 02215.

Backlar, P. (1994). The Family Face of Schizophrenia. New York: Tarcher/Putnam.

Bernheim, K., Lewine, R, & Beale, C. (1982). The Caring Family: Living with Chronic Mental Illness. New York: Random House.

Moorman, M. (1992). My Sister's Keeper. New York: W. W. Norton.

Stein, E. (1994). Straitjacket & Tie. New York: Ticknor & Fields.

Torney, Carrie Lyn (1994). What's Wrong With Nick? (explains Mental Illness to children). Friends of Nick, P.O. Box 972, Claremont, N.H.

Woolis, R. (1992). When Someone You Love Has a Mental Illness: A Handbook. New York: Tarcher/Perigree Books.

Torrey, E. Fuller (1988). Surviving Schizophrenia: A Manual for Families. New York: Harper & Row.

Carlisle, W. (1984). Siblings of the Mentally Ill. CA: R&E Publishers.

Brown, E. (1989). My Parent's Keeper: Adult Children of the Emotionally Disturbed. Oakland, CA. New Harbinger.

Johnson, J. (1989). Understanding Mental Illness (A Book for Teens). Minneapolis: Lerner.

Dinner, S. (1989). Nothing To Be Ashamed of: Growing Up With Mental Illness in Your Family. New York: Lothrop, Lee, and Shepard.

Podell, Martin. Contagious Emotions. (1992). New York: Pocket Books.

Wender, Paul & Klein, Donald. (1982). Mind, Mood, & Medicine. New York: Meridian.

Wilson, C. (1992). I Promised My Dad. New York: Simon & Schuster.

Johnson, J. (1988). Hidden Victims. New York: Doubleday.

ABOUT THE AUTHOR

Mary Brust Heaney observes and records the world of mental illness from her perspective as wife and assistant of psychiatrist Joseph A. Heaney, M.D. Her essays and poems appear regularly in the Wisconsin Psychiatric Association Newsletter. She has written numerous magazine articles and edits a newsletter in Cumberland, Wisconsin where she and her husband live. They have six children.